AMERICA'S SECRET WEAPON

The Navajo Code Talkers of World War II

BY HOWARD GUTNER

CELEBRATION PRESS
Pearson Learning Group

CONTENTS

DANGER ISLAND

The island of Saipan, smaller than some American cities, is a tiny dot in the western Pacific Ocean. The landscape is harsh. Steep mountains drop off suddenly into deep canyons. In some places, the plant growth is so thick it's almost impossible to walk.

No soldier would choose to fight a war on Saipan. However, the village of Garapan on this small island has one of the best harbors in the central Pacific. During World War II, the harbor was controlled by Japanese soldiers. American forces landed there in June 1944, determined to capture the harbor and all of Saipan as well.

Navajo code talker Carl Gorman on a lookout post overlooking Garapan on the island of Saipan

The fighting went on for weeks as each side rained deadly shells on the opposing forces. The land was so rugged and the battles were so fierce that the invading U.S. Marines gave nicknames such as "Death Valley" to parts of the island.

One morning, a **battalion** of U.S. Marines scouting the enemy front was greeted by an unusual silence. As they moved toward the enemy territory, they saw that Japanese troops had left that area and moved to a new position.

Then, a blast ripped through the jungle. The marines ducked for cover as dirt and branches flew through the air.

The gunfire went on. The soldiers soon realized that the shells were coming from their own side. American gunners didn't know that the Japanese forces had pulled out of the area. They thought they were firing at the enemy.

One of the marines quickly made his way to the radio. He sent an urgent message to headquarters, asking them to hold their fire.

The battalion didn't know that headquarters had been getting phony messages from the Japanese troops. Many enemy soldiers had learned to speak perfect English. The officers at the marines' headquarters thought the message was fake! Shells continued to explode.

Once again, a soldier from the battalion got on the radio and begged headquarters to stop the shelling. Headquarters came back with an odd question. "Do you have a Navajo?"

This battalion did have a Navajo soldier. He got on the radio right away and began sending a message in code. The code was based on the Navajo language.

Back at headquarters, another Navajo soldier took the message and decoded it. He gave it to the officers. This time, the officers knew the message really came from the marines. They stopped the shelling. There was no way the enemy could have sent the message. Why? Because this code had never been broken by the Japanese.

The Navajo "code talkers" took part in every battle that the marines conducted in the Pacific from 1942 to 1945. Over and over again, they saved American lives. About 400 code talkers served in the marines. They were among the thousands of Native American people who served in the war.

Code talkers sent messages from Pacific beaches and from trenches deep in jungles. They did their work while bullets whistled past them and bombs exploded. The code talkers were America's secret weapon, and the weapon they used was their own Navajo language.

THE NAVAJOS AND THE U.S. GOVERNMENT

The Navajo people were not strangers to war. About 80 years before the beginning of World War II, they had fought the government of the United States—and lost.

The Navajos came from a group of people who once made their homes in what is now Alaska and Canada. Hundreds of years ago they moved south. They settled in lands that would eventually become the states of Arizona, New Mexico, and Utah. Because they were scattered over such a wide area, the Navajos did not have leaders that ruled the entire Navajo nation.

In the 1840s, white settlers began to move into Navajo territory. The Navajo people tried to drive them away. U.S. officials tried to bargain with the Navajos to leave the settlers in peace, but they didn't know Navajo ways. When they signed a treaty with local Navajo leaders, they assumed the entire nation would follow its rules. But Navajos who had not read or signed a specific treaty saw no reason to follow it. There were many clashes between the U.S. government and the Navajos.

The fighting went on for years. Then, in 1864, the

Navajos made a last stand against the U.S. cavalry. Colonel Kit Carson and his soldiers began destroying the Navajos' crops, livestock, and homes. Faced with starvation, the Navajos had no choice but to give in.

The soldiers then forced about 8,000 Navajos to leave their homeland and travel on foot to a reservation near Fort Sumner, New Mexico. As a result, hundreds of Navajos died from starvation and illness. Some died on the journey, which is known in Navajo history as the Long Walk. Others died in captivity on the reservation.

A treaty signed in 1868 established a new Navajo reservation in their former territory. The Navajos returned, but they never forgot the Long Walk. Stories of their suffering were passed on from one generation to the next.

Symbols recorded by Navajos in a New Mexico canyon tell of their treatment at Kit Carson's hands.

A Navajo woman weaving near her home in the early 1900s

In the years that followed, the Navajo people had new problems with the U.S. government. Many Navajos made a living raising sheep and weaving blankets, rugs, and clothing from the wool. However, the government decided that raising so many grazing sheep was destroying the land. In the 1930s, they removed or killed thousands of sheep. The Navajos were devastated.

Why, then, did the Navajos decide to help defend the United States in wartime? In their view, fighting to defend America was equal to fighting to defend their own homeland. In 1918, when America had entered World War I, many Navajos and other Native Americans had joined the armed forces. In fact, it was during World War I that the first Native American languages were used to make wartime codes.

THE BIRTH OF AN IDEA

Sending messages between army groups has always been dangerous. If the message falls into enemy hands, an important battle could be lost.

More than 2,000 years ago, the Roman general Julius Caesar invented a secret code to send messages within his army. The code became known as the Caesar **cipher**.

In this code, each letter in an alphabet stands for another letter. Caesar's code replaced each letter in a message with another one three positions down in the Latin alphabet. In English, the word *cipher* would become *flskhu* using the Caesar cipher. A message written in a type of code is known as a **cryptogram**. Variations of the cryptogram were used to send military messages for centuries. In some versions, code words replaced names and locations.

In 1863, however, Prussian Army officer Friedrich Kasiski developed a system that could break almost any cryptogram. This system, the "Kasiski Test," looks at sets of letters that often appear together, such as *the* or *-ed*. The test also considers which letters, such as *e* and *t*, appear in words most frequently. As the Kasiski Test became well known, armies had to find new ways to code messages.

A group of Choctaw code talkers. Their commanding officer is at far right.

Codes that were easily broken were a major problem for American troops in World War I. By 1918, as the Germans dug into a position in France, the problem had reached a crisis. The Americans knew that the Germans had broken the U.S. codes and tapped their phone lines.

An American commander named Captain Lawrence was walking among his troops one night in France when he heard some soldiers talking. They were speaking to each other in their native Choctaw language. He called one of the men over and asked how many Choctaws were in their battalion. There were eight. Captain Lawrence quickly **enlisted** them as radio messengers.

The Choctaw soldiers sent messages to each other back and forth over telephone lines. They also wrote messages in Choctaw to be carried from one company to another. The German soldiers could **intercept** the messages but did not understand them. By the time three days had passed, the Germans were **retreating** from their position because they couldn't break the code.

After World War I, the Germans were able to recognize the Choctaw language as the basis for the secret code. They did not want to be fooled again. In the 1920s and 1930s many German students visited Native American reservations to learn Native American languages.

By 1941, when America entered World War II, the Germans had studied almost all the Native American nations and their languages. However, they never studied the Navajos. In fact, in 1940, only a few dozen people outside the Navajo nation could understand their language. One man who did, however, would use it to change the course of World War II.

Philip Johnston's desire to help the war effort began after the Japanese attacked Pearl Harbor. On December 7, 1941, hundreds of Japanese warplanes had roared over the U.S. base at Pearl Harbor, Hawaii. They bombed American ships and planes, and the attack drew the United States into World War II.

People all over the country reacted in shock to the attack. Philip Johnston, who lived in California, was a veteran of World War I. In 1941, he was too old to fight in the armed forces. Still, he wanted to find a way to help his country win the war. Not long after Pearl Harbor was bombed, Johnston read a news story about an Army division that was trying out codes in Native American languages. Johnston had an idea. Why not invent a code using the Navajo language?

Johnston worked as an engineer in Los Angeles. He lived far from the Navajo people. He knew a great deal about them, though. His parents had been missionaries to the Navajos. Johnston had spent most of his childhood living among Navajo people. He was one of the few non-Navajos in the world who could speak their language **fluently**.

In February 1942, Johnston traveled to Camp Elliot, near San Diego, California. He wanted to present his idea to the U.S. Marines. At first, they weren't interested.

Johnston spoke to an officer named James Jones. Jones told him the idea wouldn't work. For one thing, they knew all about the German students who had studied Native American languages. Johnston argued that the Navajo language was different from other

Philip Johnston, photographed during a recruiting tour of the Navajo reservation

Native American languages. It was extremely hard to learn. Unlike the Cherokee language, for example, Navajo had no alphabet. Except for a few notes made by scholars, the language was only spoken, not written down. It was passed on orally from one generation to another. The meaning of a word also changed depending on the **pitch** of the speaker's voice.

What's more, Johnston said, the language was always changing as new words were added. It didn't matter if Navajos had no words for military terms such as *bomb* and *tank*. They could make up words for those terms.

Jones said that Johnston's idea was worth a try. On February 28, 1942, Johnston gave a demonstration. He brought four Navajos to Camp Elliot and sent them into different offices. They talked by radio, translating messages from English to Navajo and back.

A general named Clayton Vogel saw the demonstration and was convinced. In 20 seconds, the Navajos could code, send, and decode a message that took 30 minutes to send over a machine. General Vogel said that 200 Navajos should take part in the secret code project.

In May 1942, the first 29 **recruits** arrived in San Diego for basic training. Few of the young Navajos who traveled to "boot camp" had ever left the reservation before.

There was one thing the Navajos were used to, however. That was hard work under tough conditions. They thought nothing of walking for miles each day in the hot desert. Other soldiers might complain about making long hikes and having to carry heavy packs. The Navajos marched along without a word.

The new recruits did make one mistake. When their instructor told them to count in Navajo as they marched, the men quickly fell out of step and began laughing. In Navajo, "Hup, two, three, four" has no marching rhythm at all!

BUILDING THE NAVAJO CODE

Once the code talkers completed basic training, they moved to a new camp in California. There, they continued to prove themselves as tough soldiers. During one dress parade on a very hot day, some other marines fainted from the heat. The Navajos continued to stand at attention.

They began learning how to communicate messages. First, they had to learn how to take apart and put together radio equipment. When they finished, the "first 29," as they are sometimes called, were ready to begin building an unbreakable code. They were handed a list of about 200 military words and were told to come up with Navajo words that would stand for them.

This was a hard task, for many reasons. First, the Navajos had to invent words for many terms, such as *submarine* and *dive bomber*. Second, the Navajo words chosen to stand for the military terms had to be simple to pronounce. This was important because of the way Navajo is spoken. A change in pitch could change the meaning of a word. Third, the words had to be easy to memorize. The marines wouldn't be able to use code books. They couldn't risk letting the code fall into enemy hands.

The Navajos got to work. To code military terms that had no Navajo **equivalents**, they turned to nature. Many ships, for instance, were named for sea animals. A destroyer was called a *ca-lo* (shark) while a battleship was a *lo-tso* (whale). A submarine went underwater, like a fish, and was made of iron. They called it *besh-lo* (iron fish).

Airplanes were named for birds. In flight, a dive bomber made the plunging motion of a chicken hawk. The Navajo code word for *dive bomber* was *gini*, their word for *chicken hawk*. A fighter plane was *da-he-tih-hi*, for *hummingbird*.

A sample list of coded words

ENGLISH WORD	NAVAJO WORD
America	Ne-he-mah (our mother)
barrier	bih-chan-ni-ah (in the way)
battleship	lo-tso (whale)
bomb	a-ye-shi (eggs)
destroyer	ca-lo (shark)
dive bomber	gini (chicken hawk)
fighter plane	da-he-tih-hi (hummingbird)
grenades	ni-ma-si (potatoes)
observation plane	ne-as-jah (owl)
squad	debeh-li-zini (black sheep)
submarine	besh-lo (iron fish)
truck	chido-tso (big auto)

A partial listing of the Navajo code words for the English alphabet

THE NAVAJO CODE ALPHABET

Letter	English word	Navajo word
A	ant	wol-la-chee
B	bear	shush
C	cat	moasi
D	deer	be
E	elk	dzeh
F	fox	ma-e
G	goat	klizzie
H	horse	lin
I	ice	tkin
J	jaw	ah-ya-tsinne
K	kid	klizzie-yazzi
L	lamb	dibeh-yazzie
M	mouse	na-as-tso-si
N	needle	tsah
O	owl	ne-ahs-jah
P	pig	bi-so-dih
Q	quiver	ca-yeilth
R	rabbit	gah
S	sheep	dibeh
T	turkey	than-zie
U	ute	no-da-ih
V	victor	a-keh-di-glini
W	weasel	gloe-ih
X	cross	al-na-as-dzoh
Y	yucca	tsah-as-zih
Z	zinc	besh-do-tliz

In order to include more words than the original 211 military terms, the code talkers also put together an alphabet code. They took each English letter, thought of something that started with that letter, and then used the Navajo word for that object. This alphabet was needed to spell out locations, since every island and town couldn't have its own code word.

In the final code, each vowel had two or three different words. For instance, *a* was w*ol-la-chee* (*ant*), *be-la-sana* (*apple*), and *tse-nill* (*axe*). Consonants that occur frequently in English were also given several code words. These added words made it harder to find patterns in the code and break it.

Eighteen-year-old Navajo cousins Preston (left) and Frank Toledo relay orders over a radio transmitter during training to become code talkers.

Once the 29 Navajos had memorized the code, they practiced it over and over. They used the type of message that might be sent in battle. Then they tested the code in mock battles. Code-breaking experts tried to decode the messages, but they couldn't. "We couldn't even **transcribe** it, much less crack it," said one expert.

The code was approved in the late summer of 1942. When training ended that summer, two men stayed at camp to train new recruits. Philip Johnston also came to help train new code talkers. The others were put on a boat to the South Pacific. They would soon put the code to its ultimate test: combat.

LIFE IN THE WAR ZONE

The Navajo code talkers soon found that training camp was like a pleasant dream when compared to the nightmare of the South Pacific. The rainy islands could not have been more different from their desert home. They were hot and steamy. Grass could grow almost as tall as a person. This made it hard to scout for the enemy. The rivers were filled with crocodiles and leeches. The jungles had insects, lizards, and poisonous snakes.

While snakes and crocodiles could be dangerous, some encounters with wildlife in the South Pacific offered much-needed laughter.

Navajo code talkers in the South Pacific. Left to right: Oscar Ilthma, Jack Nez, Carl Gorman

The South Pacific islands were a sharp contrast to the code talkers' home in the American Southwest.

One of the men remembered a time when he and a fellow code talker were lying down in a **foxhole**. When he hung his helmet on his rifle and stuck it out of the hiding place, shots rang out. As the soldier listened to shouts and screams around him, he heard a loud thump next to him. He looked at his friend, thinking he'd been hit. Instead, he saw an enormous bullfrog sitting on his buddy's back.

Another foxhole story involves a code talker who was trying to get some sleep on the front line of battle. He felt a sudden pain and yelled out, sure that a Japanese soldier had grabbed him. Another man shined a flashlight on the back of his friend's neck and saw—a crab!

The Navajos did get some use out of the local wildlife. They were used to living off the land. They knew how to hunt, skin, and cook the animals they caught. They didn't have to live only on military **provisions**, as other soldiers did.

The men proved to be first-rate marines in the South Pacific, just as they had been in their training. The code talkers' packs were filled with heavy radio gear. Carrying the packs through the mud wasn't easy, but they managed. They were also very good at scouting at night.

For the Navajo soldiers, danger came not only from the enemy and the jungle. American soldiers sometimes mistook them for the Japanese enemy soldiers.

With their high cheekbones and dark hair and skin, the Navajos did resemble the Japanese. One code talker was even arrested while looking for a snack in a tent. Finally he talked the soldiers into taking him back to his unit. There, he was recognized as a marine.

Some units had a bodyguard protect each Navajo. This part of the code talkers' experience was dramatized in a 2002 movie called *Windtalkers*. In it, a marine is assigned to guard a young code talker. The two men become friends.

Even with bodyguards, the Navajos had highly dangerous jobs. Their first battle front was on the island of Guadalcanal.

THE CODE TALKERS HIT GUADALCANAL

On August 7, 1942, transport ships brought the U.S. Marines to Guadalcanal. It was the beginning of a grim, six-month fight to take this small island.

The airfield on Guadalcanal was very important to both sides in World War II. Whoever controlled it would control air routes to Australia. The Americans needed the airfield as a base for their planes if they wanted to drive the Japanese out of the South Pacific.

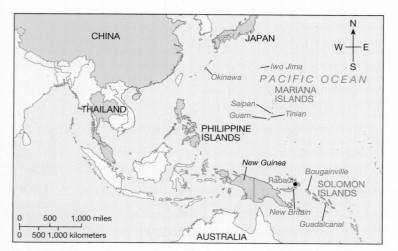

This map shows some of the major places in the Pacific (highlighted in red) in which the code talkers saw action.

Code talker Lloyd Oliver operates a field radio.

Guadalcanal taught the code talkers some key lessons. They saw how important radio communications were in the dense jungle. When groups of soldiers spread out in scouting parties, the radio was their only link to their commanders and to each other.

The code talkers also learned just how secret the code was. An early message sent by one of the talkers was overheard by marines who thought they were hearing Japanese. The soldiers began circulating wild rumors. Japanese had captured American radios! They were transmitting messages on them! Officers who were aware of the Navajo code had quite a job calming their men.

After being in actual combat, the code talkers saw that the original 211-word vocabulary was not large enough. They needed words for new military terms. Back in California, marine officers working on the Navajo code solved the problem. They almost doubled the number of words in the code.

The Navajos used some creative word play as they added to the code. For instance, the code for Adolf Hitler, the leader of Germany, was *Daghailchiih*— "Moustache Smeller." Mussolini, Italy's leader, received similar treatment. His code name was *Adee-yaats-iin Tsoh*. This meant "Big Gourd Chin."

The Japanese did eventually learn that the code existed. However, they were baffled by it. When they listened to a Navajo message, they would ask the code talker in English: "Who is this?"

At one point, they captured a Navajo Army soldier and forced him to listen to the code. The soldier knew a word here or there, but he could not figure out the code. He was able to tell his captors, truthfully, that it meant nothing to him. After the war, the Army soldier met one of the code talkers. He said, "I never figured out what you guys who got me into all that trouble were saying."

In the fall of 1943, the marines sent 11 Navajo code talkers to take over the navy's radios during action against the island of Rabaul. The island's

A bomber hits a Japanese freighter in the harbor of Rabaul island.

airfields housed hundreds of Japanese warplanes. The United States wanted to chase the Japanese off Rabaul, but they could not manage a sneak attack. The Japanese experts broke all the navy's codes.

With the code talkers in place at the radios, the navy prepared an attack. Two American air carriers launched bomber planes at the Japanese base. This time, the Japanese were taken by surprise. The bombs destroyed many of their planes and sank several of their ships. The code talkers had proved their worth, but there were even bigger victories to come.

THE CODE TALKERS' FINEST HOUR

Iwo Jima is a tiny, rocky island near the coast of Japan. During World War II, the island lay in the flight path of American B-29 planes returning to their base after bombing Japan. The Japanese fighter planes based on Iwo Jima targeted the B-29s. U.S. planes that had been struck had nowhere to land. The American bases were far away, in the Mariana Islands.

The Americans knew that if they could drive the Japanese off Iwo Jima, they would have the emergency landing field they needed and could make a safe path for their own planes. They would also have a base at which they could plan an invasion of Japan itself. The island was only about 750 miles away from the Japanese mainland. The Americans had to take Iwo Jima, and the code talkers would help them.

Japan was as determined to defend the island as the United States was to take it. Japan had placed more than 20,000 soldiers on the island. American forces had shelled the island for several months before the attack, but many Japanese soldiers had dug into positions underground.They were hidden inside a network of tunnels and caves.

The marines landed in the early morning hours of February 19, 1945. Code talker Thomas Begay remembered what it was like to arrive on the island. "The sand was ashy and hard to walk on, but I had to carry my radio and other equipment across it."

Iwo Jima saw some of the fiercest fighting of the war. The island was so important to the Japanese that they fought to defend every inch of it. They soon came out from underground and began firing at the marines.

In the middle of battle, the code talkers went to work. Six Navajo code talker units operated around the clock for the first 48 hours on Iwo Jima. With the information they sent, ships offshore were able to locate Japanese targets on land. One officer said that in those two days, the code talkers sent and received more than 800 messages with no errors.

Iwo Jima was one of the costliest battles in the Pacific. In the month of fighting, nearly 7,000 U.S. personnel lost their lives. Most were marines, including three of the code talkers. The Japanese losses were much higher. Of the thousands of Japanese soldiers on Iwo Jima, only about 1,000 survived.

On February 23, U.S. soldiers raised the American flag on top of Mount Suribachi, Iwo Jima's highest mountain. Code talkers sent the news that the mountain had been taken. They had to spell it out,

This famous statue of the flag raising on Mount Suribachi is the U.S. Marine Corps War Memorial.

letter by letter. The good news and the sight of the flag on the mountain helped give a boost to the tired Americans. They fought on for several weeks, until the entire island was in American hands. One officer said, "Were it not for the Navajos, the marines would never have taken Iwo Jima."

The code talkers and the rest of the U.S. Marines then moved on to their last Pacific front. This was the island of Okinawa, less than 400 miles from Japan's main islands. It was here that a code talker received the message in August 1945 that the Japanese had surrendered. World War II was over.

In all, thirteen code talkers died serving their country in World War II. The rest returned to their homeland. Like other returning Navajo veterans, they were welcomed as heroes by the Tribal Council and elders.

The code talkers moved on with their lives after they returned home. Some returned to their jobs. Others went to school. Some went on to become leaders in the Navajo nation.

Many were haunted by the memory of the grim sights they had seen in battle. Someone once asked code talker Lewis Ayze to describe his experiences on Saipan and Guam. He answered simply, "These stories I don't care to relate."

The veterans had been treated as equals in the armed forces. Back in Arizona, New Mexico, and Utah, voting rights for Navajos were still restricted. In many ways, however, reservation life improved after World War II. More Navajo children began to attend school. The state of Arizona finally gave Navajos the right to vote in 1948. New Mexico and Utah didn't grant Navajos voting rights until the 1950s.

Former code talkers had been told to keep the code a secret. The marines thought they might need the code again in wartime. The code was not **declassified**, or made public, until 1968. Once the word was out, the code talkers were able to talk about what they had done in the war. They began having reunions, and they formed their own association. Word of their heroism began to spread.

In 1982, President Ronald Reagan named August 14 "National Navajo Code Talkers Day." The date is the anniversary of Japan's surrender in World War II. In 1992, the code talkers were honored with an exhibit at the Pentagon. A group of the men traveled to Washington to dedicate the exhibit. During the ceremony, a code talker in Arizona phoned in a prayer for peace using the code. One of the code talkers in Washington translated the prayer. The code still worked.

Finally, in 2001, the code talkers received some long-overdue national recognition. They were given

President George W. Bush shakes hands with Congressional Gold Medal recipient John Brown Jr.

one of the nation's highest honors: the Congressional Gold and Silver Medals. The original 29 code talkers received Congressional Gold Medals in a moving ceremony. Four of the five men who were still living were able to attend. As he presented the medals, President George W. Bush said, "Today . . . we recall a story that all Americans can celebrate and every American should know." In another ceremony, silver medals were given to the group of code talkers who served later in the war.

In his speech, President Bush quoted a code talker named Albert Smith. Smith had lied about his age to join the group at age 15. Late in his life, he said, "The code word for America was 'Our Mother.' 'Our Mother' stood for freedom, our religion, our ways of life, and that's why we went in."

The Congressional Gold Medal given to the first 29 code talkers

GLOSSARY

battalion a large group of soldiers that includes a headquarters and two or more smaller military units

cipher coded message based on a key or set of rules or symbols

cryptogram a communication in code

declassified made public

enlisted engaged for duty to advance a particular cause

equivalents equals in meaning

fluently easily

foxhole a pit dug by soldiers for protection from enemy fire

intercept to seize or interrupt a communication in progress

pitch highness or lowness with which a sound is produced

provisions food supplies

recruits newly enlisted members of the armed forces

retreating making a withdrawal from a position, especially from a dangerous one

transcribe to make a written copy of something